QUOTES FOR BUSINESS

A WEEKLY JOURNAL OF QUOTES FOR
STRATEGY, GROWTH AND SUCCESS

THE QUOTIVATION SERIES

DR. JO LUKINS

Copyright © 2026 by Dr. Jo Lukins

All rights reserved.

No part of this book may be reproduced in any form or by any electronic or mechanical means, including information storage and retrieval systems, without written permission from the author, except for the use of brief quotations in a book review.

Nothing in this book creates a client or advisory relationship. The content is general in nature and is not tailored to your circumstances. It should not be used as a substitute for professional business, financial, legal, or other advice from a qualified adviser.

ISBN: 978-1-7635127-8-8 (Paperback)

Elite Edge Publishing

www.drjolukins.com

QUOTES FOR BUSINESS INVITES YOU TO EXPLORE WISDOM FROM those who have achieved in business, politics, sports, the military, and as thought leaders; thoughtfully selected to support your journey. Set aside time each week to reflect on the quote and consider what it means for you. A diary entry or reminder can help you stay committed.

This journal offers space for your weekly reflections. As you consider each quote, notice which ones resonate and which ones you might question. Both reactions help you better understand your values and approach to performance.

The second part of the book provides further reflection questions. These are designed to give you space for your own thoughts before considering additional prompts.

LOOKING FOR SOME EXTRA ACCOUNTABILITY TO KEEP YOU INSPIRED THROUGHOUT THE YEAR?

YOU CAN CHOOSE TO RECEIVE A WEEKLY EMAIL WITH EACH QUOTE AND THE JOURNAL PROMPTS TO HELP YOU STAY MOTIVATED AND ON TRACK. IF YOU'D LIKE TO RECEIVE A WEEKLY REMINDER, SIMPLY SCAN THE QR CODE BELOW AND YOU'LL START GETTING AN EMAIL WITH THE LATEST QUOTE TO HELP YOU MOVE CLOSER TO YOUR GOALS.

The quotes are organised into five key areas of successful business. If you have a particular area you'd like to focus on, use the guide below to find relevant quotes.

CUSTOMERS, RISK, INNOVATION & OPPORTUNITY:
Quotes 29, 30, 32, 33, 35, 36, 37, 39, 40, 41, 42, 43, 50, 51, 52

EXECUTION, ACTION & PRODUCTIVITY:
Quotes 8, 21, 22, 23, 24, 25, 26, 27, 28, 31

LEADERSHIP, PEOPLE & RELATIONSHIPS:
Quotes 34, 38, 44, 45, 46, 47, 48

RESILIENCE, GROWTH, MINDSET & PERSONAL MASTERY:
Quotes 1, 4, 9, 11, 12, 13, 14, 15, 16, 17, 18, 19, 20

VISION, PLANNING & STRATEGY:
Quotes 2, 3, 5, 6, 7, 10

Reflect and Perform

Each page offers a quote to spark reflection about your business mindset, routines, and team dynamics. Take your time, revisit the quote over a week, and observe how your views might change with ongoing experience.

Some quotes may be familiar, but their true value comes from thoughtful reflection. Consider how you might apply their message to make a lasting difference in your journey.

Performance-Driven Prompts

- After reflecting, what actions or habits could you apply this week in your business?
- If a quote feels at odds with your experience, notice what you believe instead, and make notes of your wisdom.

In the final section, you'll find space to add quotes you discover throughout the year, allowing your motivation to grow with you.

I look forward to sharing this journey. Reach out to let me know which quotes inspire you, and the impact they have on your performance and mindset. Shine bright, Dr. Jo (excel@drjolukins.com)

CUSTOM COPIES FOR YOUR BUSINESS, TEAM OR ORGANISATION. IF YOU'D LIKE YOUR OWN SET OF THE QUOTIVATION SERIES, PLEASE CONTACT US ABOUT CREATING A CUSTOM EDITION.

ONE

> # THE ONLY LIMIT TO OUR REALIZATION OF TOMORROW WILL BE OUR DOUBTS OF TODAY.
>
> **FRANKLIN D. ROOSEVELT**
>
> FOUR TERM US PRESIDENT, LED THROUGH THE GREAT DEPRESSION AND WORLD WAR II WITH MESSAGES OF COURAGE AND HOPE.

TWO

> # WE CANNOT CHANGE WHAT WE ARE NOT AWARE OF, AND ONCE WE ARE AWARE, WE CANNOT HELP BUT CHANGE.
>
> **SHERYL SANDBERG**
> PROMINENT TECHNOLOGY EXECUTIVE AND AUTHOR, KNOWN FOR WORK ON LEADERSHIP, GENDER EQUITY AND ORGANISATIONAL CULTURE.

THREE

THE WORLD IS CHANGING, AND WE MUST CHANGE WITH IT IF WE WANT TO STAY RELEVANT.

INDRA NOOYI

TRAILBLAZING FORMER CEO OF PEPSICO, RECOGNISED GLOBALLY FOR STRATEGIC LEADERSHIP AND TRANSFORMATIVE CHANGE IN BUSINESS.

FOUR

THE MOST SUCCESSFUL ENTREPRENEURS I KNOW ARE OPTIMISTIC. IT'S PART OF THE JOB DESCRIPTION.

CATERINA FAKE

ENTREPRENEUR AND INVESTOR, BEST KNOWN AS THE CO-FOUNDER OF FLICKR AND HUNCH, BOTH OF WHICH WERE ACQUIRED BY MAJOR TECH COMPANIES.

FIVE

> # A GOAL WITHOUT A PLAN IS JUST A WISH.
>
> **ANTOINE DE SAINT EXUPÉRY**
> CELEBRATED FRENCH WRITER AND AVIATOR, EXPLORED PURPOSE, IMAGINATION AND THE HUMAN SPIRIT IN BOTH LITERATURE AND LIFE.

SIX

A GOOD PLAN TODAY IS BETTER THAN A PERFECT PLAN TOMORROW.

GEORGE S. PATTON

INFLUENTIAL WORLD WAR II GENERAL, KNOWN FOR DECISIVE, ACTION ORIENTED LEADERSHIP UNDER PRESSURE.

SEVEN

A YEAR FROM NOW YOU WILL WISH YOU HAD STARTED TODAY.

KAREN LAMB

MOTIVATIONAL AUTHOR, WIDELY QUOTED FOR PRACTICAL INSIGHTS ON PROCRASTINATION AND TAKING TIMELY ACTION.

EIGHT

DO WHAT YOU CAN, WHERE YOU ARE, WITH WHAT YOU HAVE.

TEDDY ROOSEVELT
FORMER US PRESIDENT AND ADVENTURER, EMBODIED ENERGETIC ACTION, RESILIENCE AND PUBLIC SERVICE.

NINE

DO WHAT YOU HAVE TO DO UNTIL YOU CAN DO WHAT YOU WANT TO DO.

OPRAH WINFREY

INFLUENTIAL BROADCASTER AND
PHILANTHROPIST, RECOGNISED FOR JOURNEY
FROM ADVERSITY TO GLOBAL IMPACT.

TEN

> IF YOU CREATE AN ACT, YOU CREATE A HABIT. IF YOU CREATE A HABIT, YOU CREATE A CHARACTER. IF YOU CREATE A CHARACTER, YOU CREATE A DESTINY.
>
> **ANDRE MAUROIS**
> FRENCH BIOGRAPHER AND NOVELIST, REFLECTED DEEPLY ON CHARACTER, CHOICES AND THE STORIES PEOPLE BUILD.

ELEVEN

BUILD YOUR OWN DREAMS, OR SOMEONE ELSE WILL HIRE YOU TO BUILD THEIRS.

FARRAH GRAY
ENTREPRENEUR AND AUTHOR, BECAME A
SELF-MADE MILLIONAIRE YOUNG AND
SPEAKS ON OWNERSHIP AND AMBITION.

TWELVE

YOU CAN CHOOSE COURAGE OR YOU CAN CHOOSE COMFORT, BUT YOU CANNOT HAVE BOTH.

BRENE BROWN

RESEARCH PROFESSOR AND STORYTELLER, WORK ON VULNERABILITY AND COURAGE HAS INFLUENCED LEADERS WORLDWIDE.

THIRTEEN

FAILURE IS NOT THE OPPOSITE OF SUCCESS; IT IS PART OF SUCCESS.

ARIANNA HUFFINGTON

MEDIA ENTREPRENEUR AND AUTHOR, ADVOCATES FOR REDEFINING SUCCESS TO INCLUDE WELLBEING AND RECOVERY.

FOURTEEN

DO NOT BE EMBARRASSED BY YOUR FAILURES, LEARN FROM THEM AND START AGAIN.

RICHARD BRANSON

FOUNDER OF THE VIRGIN GROUP, KNOWN FOR ADVENTUROUS ENTREPRENEURSHIP AND LEARNING THROUGH EXPERIMENTATION.

FIFTEEN

IF YOU REALLY LOOK CLOSELY, MOST OVERNIGHT SUCCESSES TOOK A LONG TIME.

STEVE JOBS

CO FOUNDER OF APPLE, SYNONYMOUS WITH DESIGN LED INNOVATION AND RELENTLESS PURSUIT OF EXCELLENCE.

SIXTEEN

> # SUCCESS IS WALKING FROM FAILURE TO FAILURE WITH NO LOSS OF ENTHUSIASM.
>
> **WINSTON CHURCHILL**
> BRITISH WARTIME PRIME MINISTER, EMBLEMATIC OF PERSEVERANCE AND RESOLVE DURING CRISES.

SEVENTEEN

PROFIT IS APPLAUSE FOR SOLVING A REAL PROBLEM.

WHITNEY JOHNSON

CEO OF DISRUPTION ADVISORS, A LEADERSHIP DEVELOPMENT FIRM; BESTSELLING AUTHOR ON PERSONAL DISRUPTION AND GROWTH.

EIGHTEEN

DON'T LET WHAT YOU CANNOT DO INTERFERE WITH WHAT YOU CAN DO.

JOHN WOODEN

LEGENDARY BASKETBALL COACH, ADMIRED FOR VALUES BASED COACHING AND LIFELONG LEARNING.

NINETEEN

HALF OF GETTING WHAT YOU WANT IS KNOWING WHAT YOU HAVE TO GIVE UP TO GET IT.

BILL PHILLIPS

FITNESS AUTHOR AND ENTREPRENEUR, FOCUSES ON DISCIPLINED CHANGE AND TRADE OFFS IN PURSUIT OF GOALS.

TWENTY

> # I ATTRIBUTE MY SUCCESS TO THIS: I NEVER GAVE OR TOOK ANY EXCUSE.
>
> **FLORENCE NIGHTINGALE**
>
> FOUNDER OF MODERN NURSING, REDEFINED HEALTHCARE THROUGH DATA, DISCIPLINE AND COMPASSIONATE SERVICE.

TWENTY-ONE

> TO ACHIEVE GREAT THINGS, TWO THINGS ARE NEEDED; A PLAN, AND NOT QUITE ENOUGH TIME.
> **LEONARD BERNSTEIN**
> RENOWNED CONDUCTOR/COMPOSER OF THE NEW YORK PHILHARMONIC, CELEBRATED FOR WEST SIDE STORY & HIS INFLUENCE AS A GLOBAL CLASSICAL MUSIC EDUCATOR.

TWENTY-TWO

LUCK HAS NOTHING TO DO WITH IT, BECAUSE I HAVE SPENT MANY, MANY HOURS, COUNTLESS HOURS, ON THE COURT WORKING FOR MY ONE MOMENT IN TIME.

SERENA WILLIAMS

ONE OF THE GREATEST TENNIS PLAYERS IN HISTORY, EXEMPLIFIES DISCIPLINED PREPARATION AND COMPETITIVE RESILIENCE.

TWENTY-THREE

TO BE SUCCESSFUL, YOU DON'T HAVE TO DO EXTRAORDINARY THINGS. JUST DO ORDINARY THINGS EXTRAORDINARILY WELL.

JOHN ROHN

BUSINESS PHILOSOPHER AND SPEAKER, INFLUENCED GENERATIONS OF ENTREPRENEURS WITH FOCUS ON DAILY DISCIPLINES.

TWENTY-FOUR

DONE IS BETTER THAN PERFECT.

SHERYL SANDBERG

PROMINENT TECHNOLOGY EXECUTIVE AND AUTHOR, ENCOURAGES BIAS FOR ACTION OVER PERFECTIONISM IN FAST MOVING ENVIRONMENTS.

TWENTY-FIVE

DON'T SIT DOWN AND WAIT FOR THE OPPORTUNITIES TO COME. GET UP AND MAKE THEM.

MADAM C.J. WALKER

PIONEERING ENTREPRENEUR AND PHILANTHROPIST, BECAME ONE OF THE FIRST SELF MADE FEMALE MILLIONAIRES IN AMERICA.

TWENTY-SIX

DON'T WATCH THE CLOCK; DO WHAT IT DOES. KEEP GOING.

SAM LEVENSON

AMERICAN HUMORIST AND TEACHER, USED WIT TO HIGHLIGHT PERSISTENCE AND EVERYDAY WISDOM.

TWENTY-SEVEN

> BUSINESS IS LIKE RIDING A BICYCLE. EITHER YOU KEEP MOVING OR YOU FALL DOWN.
>
> **JOHN DAVID WRIGHT**
>
> BUSINESS COMMENTATOR AND WRITER, KNOWN FOR PRACTICAL REFLECTIONS ON MOMENTUM AND ADAPTABILITY IN WORK.

TWENTY-EIGHT

IT TAKES 20 YEARS TO BUILD A REPUTATION AND FIVE MINUTES TO RUIN IT.

WARREN BUFFETT

LEGENDARY INVESTOR AND BUSINESS LEADER, WIDELY RESPECTED FOR LONG TERM THINKING AND INTEGRITY.

TWENTY-NINE

> # THE MOST DIFFICULT THING IS THE DECISION TO ACT, THE REST IS MERELY TENACITY.
>
> **AMELIA EARHART**
> AVIATION PIONEER, BROKE BARRIERS IN FLIGHT AND BECAME A SYMBOL OF COURAGE AND EXPLORATION.

THIRTY

> # THE QUESTION ISN'T WHO IS GOING TO LET ME; IT'S WHO IS GOING TO STOP ME.
>
> **AYN RAND**
>
> NOVELIST AND PHILOSOPHER, KNOWN FOR ADVOCACY OF INDIVIDUALISM, AGENCY AND DARING ENTERPRISE.

THIRTY-ONE

IF YOU CAN'T MEASURE IT, YOU CAN'T IMPROVE IT.

PETER DRUCKER

INFLUENTIAL MANAGEMENT THINKER, EMPHASISED CLEAR OBJECTIVES, MEASUREMENT AND LEARNING IN ORGANISATIONS.

THIRTY-TWO

A SATISFIED CUSTOMER IS THE BEST BUSINESS STRATEGY OF ALL.

MICHAEL LEBOEUF

BUSINESS AUTHOR AND CONSULTANT, FOCUSES ON CUSTOMER DRIVEN PERFORMANCE AND PRACTICAL MANAGEMENT.

THIRTY-THREE

YOUR MOST UNHAPPY CUSTOMERS ARE YOUR GREATEST SOURCE OF LEARNING.

BILL GATES

CO FOUNDER OF MICROSOFT & PHILANTHROPIST, STRESSES FEEDBACK, DATA AND CONTINUOUS IMPROVEMENT.

THIRTY-FOUR

> BUSINESS IS ALL ABOUT RELATIONSHIPS, HOW WELL YOU BUILD THEM DETERMINES HOW WELL THEY BUILD YOUR BUSINESS.

BRAD SUGARS

ENTREPRENEUR AND BUSINESS EDUCATOR, HAS COACHED LEADERS WORLDWIDE ON GROWTH THROUGH SYSTEMS AND PEOPLE.

THIRTY-FIVE

THE CUSTOMER'S PERCEPTION IS YOUR REALITY.

KATE ZABRISKIE

CUSTOMER SERVICE TRAINER AND AUTHOR, SPECIALISES IN COMMUNICATION AND CLIENT EXPERIENCE.

THIRTY-SIX

> # IN THE MIDDLE OF DIFFICULTY LIES OPPORTUNITY.
>
> **ALBERT EINSTEIN**
> PIONEERING PHYSICIST, REVOLUTIONISED SCIENCE AND OFTEN REFLECTED ON CURIOSITY AND CREATIVE PROBLEM SOLVING.

THIRTY-SEVEN

IT'S NOT THE STRONGEST OF THE SPECIES THAT SURVIVE, NOR THE MOST INTELLIGENT, BUT THE ONE MOST RESPONSIVE TO CHANGE.

CHARLES DARWIN

NATURALIST AND SCIENTIST, THEORY OF EVOLUTION UNDERPINS MODERN UNDERSTANDING OF ADAPTATION AND SURVIVAL.

THIRTY-EIGHT

A RISING TIDE RAISES ALL BOATS.

JOHN F. KENNEDY

FORMER US PRESIDENT, REMEMBERED FOR ASPIRATIONAL LEADERSHIP AND A FOCUS ON SHARED PROSPERITY.

THIRTY-NINE

> # BUSINESS OPPORTUNITIES ARE LIKE BUSES, THERE'S ALWAYS ANOTHER ONE COMING.

RICHARD BRANSON

ENTREPRENEUR AND FOUNDER OF VIRGIN, KNOWN FOR SEIZING OPPORTUNITIES ACROSS DIVERSE INDUSTRIES.

FORTY

IF THE WIND WILL NOT SERVE, TAKE TO THE OARS.

LATIN PROVERB

TRADITIONAL PROVERB THAT CAPTURES RESOURCEFULNESS AND SELF DRIVEN ACTION NO MATTER THE CONDITIONS.

FORTY-ONE

THE PERSON WHO SAYS IT CANNOT BE DONE SHOULD NOT INTERRUPT THE PERSON WHO IS DOING IT.

CHINESE PROVERB

POPULAR PROVERB EMPHASISING INITIATIVE, ACTION AND CONSTRUCTIVE FOCUS OVER CRITICISM.

FORTY-TWO

TO AVOID CRITICISM, SAY NOTHING, DO NOTHING, BE NOTHING.

ARISTOTLE

INFLUENTIAL GREEK PHILOSOPHER, SHAPED THINKING ON ETHICS, LOGIC, POLITICS AND THE EXAMINED LIFE.

FORTY-THREE

YOU MUST ALWAYS BE ABLE TO PREDICT WHAT IS NEXT AND THEN HAVE THE FLEXIBILITY TO EVOLVE.

MARC BENIOFF

FOUNDER AND CEO OF SALESFORCE
KNOWN FOR CLOUD INNOVATION AND
VALUES DRIVEN CORPORATE LEADERSHIP.

FORTY-FOUR

> A LEADER IS ANYONE WHO TAKES RESPONSIBILITY FOR FINDING THE POTENTIAL IN PEOPLE AND PROCESSES, AND WHO HAS THE COURAGE TO DEVELOP THAT POTENTIAL.
>
> **RALPH NADER**
> CONSUMER ADVOCATE AND POLITICAL REFORMER, HAS SPENT DECADES CHALLENGING SYSTEMS AND CHAMPIONING ACCOUNTABILITY.

FORTY-FIVE

> # LEADERSHIP IS NOT ABOUT BEING IN CHARGE. IT'S ABOUT TAKING CARE OF THOSE IN YOUR CHARGE.
>
> **SIMON SINEK**
>
> BESTSELLING AUTHOR AND SPEAKER, KNOWN FOR WORK ON PURPOSE DRIVEN LEADERSHIP AND TRUST IN ORGANISATIONS.

FORTY-SIX

ALWAYS BE MORE THAN YOU APPEAR AND NEVER APPEAR TO BE MORE THAN YOU ARE.

ANGELA MERKEL

LONG SERVING GERMAN CHANCELLOR RESPECTED FOR STEADY, PRAGMATIC LEADERSHIP ON THE GLOBAL STAGE.

FORTY-SEVEN

THE WORLD IS CHANGED BY YOUR EXAMPLE, NOT BY YOUR OPINION.

PAULO COELHO

INTERNATIONALLY RENOWNED NOVELIST WRITES ABOUT MEANING, COURAGE AND FOLLOWING A PERSONAL PATH.

FORTY-EIGHT

WHENEVER YOU SEE A SUCCESSFUL BUSINESS, SOMEONE ONCE MADE A COURAGEOUS DECISION.

PETER DRUCKER

OFTEN CALLED THE FATHER OF MODERN MANAGEMENT, SHAPED HOW ORGANISATIONS THINK ABOUT STRATEGY AND EFFECTIVENESS.

FORTY-NINE

IT IS LITERALLY TRUE THAT YOU CAN SUCCEED BEST AND QUICKEST BY HELPING OTHERS TO SUCCEED.

NAPOLEON HILL

INFLUENTIAL SUCCESS WRITER, STUDIED HIGH PERFORMERS AND POPULARISED PRINCIPLES OF MINDSET AND MUTUAL BENEFIT.

FIFTY

> # THE ROAD TO SUCCESS AND THE ROAD TO FAILURE ARE ALMOST EXACTLY THE SAME.
>
> **COLIN R. DAVIS**
> ACCLAIMED CONDUCTOR, LED MAJOR ORCHESTRAS AND UNDERSTOOD PERFORMANCE, RISK AND INTERPRETATION AT THE HIGHEST LEVEL.

FIFTY-ONE

RISK MORE THAN OTHERS THINK IS SAFE. DREAM MORE THAN OTHERS THINK IS PRACTICAL.

HOWARD SCHULTZ

FORMER STARBUCKS CEO, SCALED A GLOBAL BRAND BY BLENDING EXPERIENCE DESIGN, CULTURE AND BOLD EXPANSION.

FIFTY-TWO

THE DIFFERENCE BETWEEN SUCCESSFUL PEOPLE AND VERY SUCCESSFUL PEOPLE IS THAT VERY SUCCESSFUL PEOPLE SAY 'NO' TO ALMOST EVERYTHING.

WARREN BUFFETT

RENOWNED INVESTOR, HIGHLIGHTS FOCUS AND SELECTIVE DECISION MAKING AS KEYS TO SUSTAINED SUCCESS.

You'll find my reflection questions in the following section. They've been included separately so you can first explore your own ideas and see what stands out to you.

This is your opportunity to stretch your thinking, challenge your habits, and connect each concept to your training and performance in a real and personal way.

Once you've completed your initial reflections, take a moment to read through the additional questions. See what sparks your curiosity or pushes you to think differently. Go back to your earlier notes and build on them; this is where real growth happens.

This process is designed to help you get the most from your reflections and keep your focus on progress, not perfection. Your effort in this space will be reflected in how you show up in your leadership and your life.

DR. JO

ONE

 The only limit to our realization of tomorrow will be our doubts of today.

FRANKLIN D. ROOSEVELT

Self-doubt can quietly restrict ambition more than external barriers ever do. By challenging limiting beliefs now, you expand what becomes possible in your future.

- What doubt is currently holding you back?
- What evidence do you have that contradicts that doubt?
- What action today would show belief in your future?

TWO

 We cannot change what we are not aware of, and once we are aware, we cannot help but change.

SHERYL SANDBERG

Awareness is the starting point of any meaningful change. Once a pattern becomes clear, it naturally creates pressure to act differently.

- What important truth about yourself/your work are you avoiding noticing?
- Where have you recently become more aware, and how has that shifted you?
- What is one change you will make now?

THREE

 The world is changing, and we must change with it if we want to stay relevant.

INDRA NOOYI

Relevance is not permanent; it must be earned through continual adaptation. Staying still in a changing world is effectively moving backwards.

- Where in your life or business are you resisting change?
- What trend or shift do you most need to respond to?
- How will you ensure you keep learning rather than clinging to past success?

FOUR

 All great achievements require time.

MAYA ANGELOU

Meaningful work and lasting accomplishment cannot be rushed. The depth of what you build is directly tied to the patience and sustained effort you invest.

- What achievement matters most to you, and how long are you willing to invest?
- Where are you pressuring yourself to achieve faster than the work requires?
- How can you trust the timeline your goals actually need?

FIVE

 A goal without a plan is just a wish.

ANTOINE DE SAINT EXUPÉRY

Desire alone does not create outcomes; structure and planning do. Turning a wish into reality requires clarity, steps, and accountability.

- Which of your current wishes needs to become a concrete plan?
- What is the first actionable step in that plan?
- Who or what will help you stay on track?

SIX

 A good plan today is better than a perfect plan tomorrow.

GEORGE S. PATTON

Timely, imperfect action usually beats delayed perfection. Momentum and learning from doing matter more than endless preparation. Striving for perfection typically ends in failure.

- Where are you waiting for the perfect plan before you begin?
- What could you launch or test with a good-enough plan right now?
- What might you learn only by starting?

SEVEN

 A year from now you will wish you had started today

KAREN LAMB

Procrastination steals future satisfaction. The progress you want to see in a year depends on choices you make today.

- If you started today, what could be different in 12 months?
- What task have you been postponing that future-you will thank you for starting?
- What is the smallest action you can take in the next 24 hours?

EIGHT

 Do what you can, where you are, with what you have.

TEDDY ROOSEVELT

Resourcefulness matters more than excuses. You are encouraged to begin with your current tools, location, and capacity; power lies in action, not ideal conditions.

- What are you underestimating in your current resources?
- Where are you waiting for more instead of using what you have?
- How can you make meaningful progress from exactly where you are?

NINE

 Do what you have to do until you can do what you want to do.

OPRAH WINFREY

Sometimes duty and discipline precede freedom and choice. Doing necessary work now lays the foundation for doing desired work later.

- What need-to tasks are instrumental to your want-to life?
- How can purpose assist the routine parts of your work?
- What future freedom are you building by showing up today?

TEN

 If you create an act, you create a habit If you create a habit, you create a character If you create a character, you create a destiny.

ANDRE MAUROIS

Daily habits are the foundation of our success. Your daily choices quietly sculpt who you become, habits never lie.

- Which daily act is currently shaping your future most?
- What habit do you need to break because it does not fit your desired destiny?
- What new habit would better align with the person you want to be?

ELEVEN

 Build your own dreams, or someone else will hire you to build theirs.

FARRAH GRAY

Ownership of your goals is a conscious choice. If you don't pursue your own vision, your energy will be spent advancing someone else's.

- Whose dreams are you mostly building right now?
- What does building your own dream practically look like this week?
- What risk or decision would move you closer to your vision?

TWELVE

 You can choose courage or you can choose comfort, but you cannot have both.

BRENÉ BROWN

Growth and bravery rarely coexist with comfort. Choosing courage means accepting vulnerability and uncertainty.

- Where are you choosing comfort over courage?
- What courageous conversation or action are you avoiding?
- How might your life change if you tolerated more discomfort in service of growth?

THIRTEEN

 Failure is not the opposite of success; it is part of success.

ARIANNA HUFFINGTON

Failure is an essential ingredient of success rather than its opposite. Each setback provides data, resilience, and refinement.

- How do you usually interpret your failures?
- What is one lesson a recent failure is offering you?
- How would you act differently if you truly believed failure was progress?

FOURTEEN

 Do not be embarrassed by your failures, learn from them and start again.

RICHARD BRANSON

Recovering quickly and constructively from mistakes matters more than sitting in regret. Reflection plus renewed action is more powerful than embarrassment.

- Where are you still stuck in shame instead of learning?
- What did your last setback teach you about your approach or strategy?
- What is your start again step from here?

FIFTEEN

 If you really look closely, most overnight successes took a long time.

STEVE JOBS

The myth of overnight success masks years of unseen effort. Persistence behind the scenes creates visible results.

- Whose overnight success are you comparing yourself to unfairly?
- What long-term work of yours remains unseen but valuable?
- How can you recommit to the process rather than the spotlight?

SIXTEEN

 Success is walking from failure to failure with no loss of enthusiasm.

WINSTON CHURCHILL

Success can be seen as the ability to keep your spirit alive despite repeated setbacks. Enthusiasm becomes a renewable fuel that carries you through disappointment.

- Where have you recently lost enthusiasm after a setback?
- What helps you emotionally reset so you can keep going?
- How can you protect your energy while still persisting?

SEVENTEEN

 Great works are performed not by strength but by perseverance.

SAMUEL JOHNSON

Lasting achievement grows from sustained effort more than raw talent or power. Consistent, determined action compounds over time.

- Which of your goals requires perseverance more than a single burst of effort?
- How do you maintain effort when progress slows?
- Where could you recommit to steady, long-term dedication?

EIGHTEEN

 Don't let what you cannot do interfere with what you can do.

JOHN WOODEN

Shifting attention from limitations to possibilities accelerates progress. Energy invested in what is within your control produces better outcomes than dwelling on what is not.

- What current limitation are you dwelling on too much?
- What can you do today despite that limitation?
- How would your results change if you focused only on your controllables?

NINETEEN

 Half of getting what you want is knowing what you have to give up to get it.

BILL PHILLIPS

Gains usually require trade-offs. Clarity about what you are willing to sacrifice sharpens your commitment to your goals.

- Which of your goals need a trade-off decision?
- What habit, comfort, or distraction must you release to move forward?
- What is the price for getting what you want?

TWENTY

 I attribute my success to this: I never gave or took any excuse.

FLORENCE NIGHTINGALE

Progress comes from refusing to blame circumstances or others. Letting go of excuses frees energy for focused action.

- Where are you currently making excuses instead of decisions?
- What would a key area of your life be like without excuses?
- What support or structure would help you live this standard?

TWENTY-ONE

 You may be disappointed if you fail, but you are doomed if you don't try.

BEVERLY SILLS

Risk and possible failure are inherent in meaningful action. Choosing not to try guarantees nothing; an attempt makes success possible.

- Where are you playing it too safe instead of trying?
- What would you attempt if you accepted the possibility of disappointment?
- How can you reframe trying as a win regardless of outcome?

TWENTY-TWO

 Luck has nothing to do with it, because I have spent many, many hours, countless hours, on the court working for my one moment in time.

SERENA WILLIAMS

So-called luck is often the visible moment built on countless hours of practice. Preparation creates the conditions for opportunities.

- In what area do you wish for luck but lack preparation?
- What daily discipline would significantly raise your chances of success?
- How can you best invest the time that is needed?

TWENTY-THREE

 To be successful, you don't have to do extraordinary things. Just do ordinary things extraordinarily well

JOHN ROHN

Excellence often lies in mastering fundamentals rather than chasing perfection. Consistent high standards in simple tasks compounds into success.

- Which are the key consistent basic behaviours needed in your work?
- How could you bring more care and quality to routine?
- Where might extraordinary results come from better execution, rather than new ideas?

TWENTY-FOUR

 Done is better than perfect.

SHERYL SANDBERG

Perfectionism can paralyse progress. Completing meaningful work, even imperfectly, creates momentum and learning.

- Where are you stuck polishing instead of completing?
- What project would benefit most from being finished rather than perfect?
- What good-enough criteria could help you move forward faster?

TWENTY-FIVE

 Don't sit down and wait for the opportunities to come. Get up and make them.

MADAM C.J. WALKER

Proactive behaviour is more powerful than passive waiting. Initiative and action attract chances that would not appear on their own.

- Where are you waiting for permission or an invitation?
- What opportunity could you create for you this week?
- Who do you need to approach rather than hoping they approach you?

TWENTY-SIX

 Don't watch the clock; do what it does Keep going.

SAM LEVENSON

Steady, forward motion is more important than constant monitoring. Consistent effort, not watching the time, leads to meaningful progress.

- How often do you watch the clock instead of working on your priorities?
- What rhythm or routine would keep you moving steadily?
- Where do you need to reduce distraction and simply keep going?

TWENTY-SEVEN

 Business is like riding a bicycle. Either you keep moving or you fall down.

JOHN DAVID WRIGHT

Balance and stability in work or business require ongoing movement. Stagnation is risky; momentum is protective.

- Is there a part of your business or work that has slowed?
- What small action could restart momentum there?
- How can you design your work to encourage continuous motion?

TWENTY-EIGHT

 It takes 20 years to build a reputation and five minutes to ruin it.

WARREN BUFFETT

Trust is fragile: building it is slow, but damaging it is quick and sometimes irreversible. Guarding integrity becomes a strategic necessity.

- What behaviours most influence your reputation right now?
- Where might you be taking trust for granted?
- What boundary or standard do you need to strengthen to protect your name?

TWENTY-NINE

 The most difficult thing is the decision to act, the rest is merely tenacity.

AMELIA EARHART

Beginning is usually the hardest part; once committed, persistence becomes simpler and more mechanical. Courage concentrates in the initial decision.

- On what important action are you delaying making a decision?
- What fears are blocking that decision?
- What would you choose today if you trusted your call?

THIRTY

 The question isn't who is going to let me; it's who is going to stop me.

AYN RAND

Embrace a mindset of self-determination and independence. Attention shifts from seeking approval to strengthening inner resolve.

- Where are you unconsciously seeking others' permission?
- What project would you pursue differently if you assumed no one could stop you?
- How can you strengthen your own conviction in your decisions?

THIRTY-ONE

 If you can't measure it, you can't improve it.

PETER DRUCKER

Improvement requires clarity and feedback. Without concrete measures, performance remains vague and progress becomes guesswork.

- Which important goal of yours is currently unmeasured?
- What simple metric could show whether you are improving?
- How often will you review your key numbers?

THIRTY-TWO

 A satisfied customer is the best business strategy of all.

MICHAEL LEBOEUF

Delighted customers are not just outcomes but powerful marketing assets. Their loyalty and advocacy create some of the strongest strategies for long-term success.

- How do you currently gauge your customers' satisfaction?
- What could you do this week to pleasantly surprise a customer?
- Where are you prioritising short-term gains over long-term loyalty?

THIRTY-THREE

 Your most unhappy customers are your greatest source of learning.

BILL GATES

Complaints can be the richest source of data. The most dissatisfied customers reveal gaps that, once fixed, can strengthen your business.

- How do you usually respond to complaints? Are you defensive or curious?
- What recurring criticism have you not yet addressed?
- How will you capture and use feedback with intention?

THIRTY-FOUR

 Business is all about relationships, how well you build them determines how well they build your business.

BRAD SUGARS

Success depends on the quality of your connections with clients, partners, and teams. Strong relationships generate trust, opportunities, and resilience.

- Which key relationship in your work needs attention?
- How often do you invest in relationships without expecting an immediate return?
- What behaviour of yours most strengthens or weakens trust?

THIRTY-FIVE

 The customer's perception is your reality.

KATE ZABRISKIE

What matters is less what you intend but what your client experiences. Their perception becomes the truth you must work with.

- Where might there be a gap between your intent and your customers' experience?
- How could you better understand how they actually see you or your service?
- What change would most positively shift their perception?

THIRTY-SIX

 In the middle of difficulty lies opportunity.

ALBERT EINSTEIN

Challenges often hide potential advantages or innovations. A problem reframed as a possibility can become a turning point.

- Which current difficulty could contain an unseen opportunity?
- What would you do differently if you viewed this situation as a gift?
- Who could help you see the opportunity?

THIRTY-SEVEN

 It's not the strongest of the species that survive, nor the most intelligent, but the one most responsive to change.

CHARLES DARWIN

Adaptability is a key driver of survival and success, often more important than strength or intelligence. Those who respond flexibly to new conditions tend to thrive.

- In what area are you clinging to old ways that no longer work?
- How quickly do you usually adapt when circumstances shift?
- What new skill or mindset would make you more adaptable?

THIRTY-EIGHT

 A rising tide raises all boats.

JOHN F. KENNEDY

Collective progress benefits everyone within a system. Creating broader prosperity often lifts individual outcomes at the same time.

- Where could you help raise the tide for your team or industry?
- How might others' success also support your own?
- What collaborative action could create shared benefit?

THIRTY-NINE

 Business opportunities are like buses, there's always another one coming.

RICHARD BRANSON

Missing an opportunity is not the end; more chances will appear. The key is to stay alert, prepared, and ready to act when the next arrives.

- Are you dwelling on a missed opportunity instead of preparing for the next?
- How can you be ready to act with the next opportunity?
- What criteria will help you decide which opportunities to seek?

FORTY

 If the wind will not serve, take to the oars.

LATIN PROVERB

When conditions are not favourable, self-driven effort can still move you forward. Initiative replaces waiting for perfect circumstances.

- Where are you blaming external conditions instead of prioritising action?
- What self-driven decisions could replace waiting?
- How can you build stamina for those times you must row alone?

FORTY-ONE

 The person who says it cannot be done should not interrupt the person who is doing it.

CHINESE PROVERB

This line encourages respect for doers and warns against discouraging those taking action. Skepticism and criticism are easy; contribution and effort are more valuable.

- When do you tend to criticise rather than support others' efforts?
- Who around you is doing it that you could encourage instead?
- How can you protect your own focus from people who say it cannot be done?

FORTY-TWO

 To avoid criticism, say nothing, do nothing, be nothing.

ARISTOTLE

The only way to escape criticism is to live so small that you achieve nothing. A meaningful life will inevitably attract some disapproval.

- How much does fear of criticism shape your decisions?
- Where are you shrinking to stay safe from others' opinions?
- What is worth doing even if you will be criticised?

FORTY-THREE

You must always be able to predict what is next and then have the flexibility to evolve.

MARC BENIOFF

Foresight combined with flexibility is essential for enduring success. Strategy matters, but so does the agility to adapt as reality unfolds.

- What emerging change do you most need to prepare for?
- How rigid are your current plans if conditions shift?
- What processes could help you both plan ahead and pivot quickly?

FORTY-FOUR

A leader is anyone who takes responsibility for finding the potential in people and processes, and who has the courage to develop that potential.

RALPH NADER

Leadership is framed as stewardship rather than status. How do you identify and actively develop potential in people and systems?

- Whose potential around you is underdeveloped?
- How intentionally do you look for strengths in your team or peers?
- What is one step you can take to grow someone else's capacity?

FORTY-FIVE

 Leadership is not about being in charge It's about taking care of those in your charge.

SIMON SINEK

Leadership is recast from control to service. The true role is to create safety, support, and conditions where others can do their best work.

- How well do people under your care feel supported?
- When do you prioritise being in charge over being of service?
- What concrete action could better take care of your team this week?

FORTY-SIX

 Always be more than you appear and never appear to be more than you are.

ANGELA MERKEL

Quiet substance is valued over show. The focus is on developing real competence while remaining humble and grounded.

- Where might your image be outpacing your substance?
- In what area do you want to quietly deepen your expertise?
- How can you stay grounded when others praise or overestimate you?

FORTY-SEVEN

 The world is changed by your example, not by your opinion.

PAULO COELHO

Actions influence others far more than commentary. Living your values becomes a powerful catalyst for change.

- Where are your actions not matching your stated beliefs?
- What behaviour of yours could positively inspire others this week?
- If someone copied your example today, would you be pleased with the result?

FORTY-EIGHT

 Whenever you see a successful business, someone once made a courageous decision.

PETER DRUCKER

Every successful venture began with a bold choice made in uncertainty. Progress in work or business often hinges on a single committed decision.

- What important decision are you postponing out of fear?
- What information do you truly need before deciding, and what is just stalling?
- If you were being courageous, what would you choose?

FORTY-NINE

 It is literally true that you can succeed best and quickest by helping others to succeed.

NAPOLEON HILL

A powerful path to success runs through serving others' goals. Creating value for your team builds value, opportunity, and support.

- Whose success can you meaningfully advance right now?
- How generous are you with your knowledge, network, and encouragement?
- What collaboration could turn mutual support into shared success?

FIFTY

 The road to success and the road to failure are almost exactly the same.

COLIN R. DAVIS

Success and failure often begin with similar risks and discomfort. The difference lies in persistence, learning, and adjusting along the way.

- How do you react when the road feels hard?
- How will you adapt in your next challenge?
- What small adjustment would keep you on the path toward success?

FIFTY-ONE

> Risk more than others think is safe. Dream more than others think is practical.
>
> HOWARD SCHULTZ

Vision typically requires bolder risks and more expansive dreams than most people consider reasonable. The challenge is to stretch beyond conventional safety and practicality.

- Where are your current dreams limited by what others think is practical?
- What calculated risk are you prepared to take?
- How can you better balance prudence with courage?

FIFTY-TWO

> The difference between successful people and very successful people is that very successful people say no to almost everything.
>
> WARREN BUFFETT

Success comes from clear focus rather than doing everything. Saying no to requests protects time and energy for what truly matters.

- What do you need to start saying no to more often?
- Which activities create the greatest value in your life?
- How will you guard your calendar so it reflects your real priorities?

OTHER QUOTES TO INSPIRE

Use this section to collect quotes that inspire you throughout the year. Add a few notes about why each quote stands out or what it means to you personally.

To read more from the Quotivation series

The Quotivation Series is a collection of reflective quote journals designed to take short bites of wisdom, and applying it in a practical way to your upcoming success.

Quotes for Athletes: *A weekly journal of quotes for grit, motivation and a winning mindset.*
Quotes for Coaches: *A weekly journal of quotes for leadership, motivation and excellence.*
Quotes for Referees: *A weekly journal of quotes for focus, poise and resilience.*
Quotes for Business: *A weekly journal of quotes for strategy, growth and success.*
Quotes for Leaders: *A weekly journal of quotes for vision, courage, and inspired achievement.*
Quotes for Investors: *A weekly journal of quotes for patience, clarity and a successful investors mindset.*
Quotes for Military: *A weekly journal of quotes for courage, discipline, and an unbreakable mindset in service.*
Quotes for Parenting: *A weekly journal of quotes for patience, guidance, and love.*
Quotes for Students: *A weekly journal of quotes for focus, persistence and curiosity.*
Quotes for You: *A weekly journal of quotes for growth, self-discovery, and an empowered mindset.*

The Quotivation Series is being released through 2026.
Visit my website **drjolukins.com** to be the first to order your copy or visit your preferred indie bookstore or online platform.

CUSTOM COPIES FOR YOUR TEAM OR BUSINESS

IF YOU'D LIKE TO SHARE A BOOK FROM THE QUOTIVATION SERIES WITH AN ORGANISATION, TEAM OR CLIENTS, PLEASE CONTACT US TO DISCUSS CREATING A CUSTOM EDITION.

EMAIL US AT **EXCEL@DRJOLUKINS.COM** TO FIND OUT MORE.

Read more with Dr. Jo

The following books are available at your favourite book store or online platform:

The Elite: Think like an athlete, succeed like a champion. Ten things the elite do differently. 2019

In the Grandstands: The sporting parents guide to raising a confident and happy teen in the highs and lows of youth sports. 2020

The Game Plan: Your 5-month coaching program to champion high performance habits (High Performance Thinking). 2022

The Elite and The Game Plan 2 in 1 Book: Champion your success with elite habits to unleash your winning potential with 10 proven strategies and high-performance coaching program. 2023

Belief: Building unshakeable confidence. 2024

The Whistle Blower: The mental toughness rulebook for referees, umpires, and sports officials. 2025.

The Whistle Blower Workbook: The mental toughness rulebook for referees, umpires, and sports officials. 2025

A note from Dr. Jo

Referred to as a psychological Indiana Jones, thanks to more than twenty-five years spent exploring what helps people achieve their best. I have enjoyed bringing together these quotes for you. If you'd like to connect or learn more, you can always find me at www.drjolukins.com.

If Quotes for Business has made an impact for you, I'd be grateful if you would share your thoughts or leave a review on Amazon or Goodreads. Similarly, if you'd like to share your favorite quote with me, let me know at excel@drjolukins.com

Shine Bright, Dr. Jo

www.ingramcontent.com/pod-product-compliance
Lightning Source LLC
LaVergne TN
LVHW051949060526
838201LV00059B/3578